D1483125

Making Venn
diagrams /

easy
j510H

Making Venn Diagrams

By Therese Harasymiw

Gareth Stevens
PUBLISHING

Please visit our website, www.garethstevens.com. For a free color catalog of all our high-quality books, call toll free 1-800-542-2595 or fax 1-877-542-2596.

Library of Congress Cataloging-in-Publication Data

Harasymiw, Therese.
Making Venn diagrams / by Therese Harasymiw.
p. cm. — (Graph it!)
Includes index.
ISBN 978-1-4824-0935-2 (pbk.)
ISBN 978-1-4824-0936-9 (6-pack)
ISBN 978-1-4824-0934-5 (library binding)
1. Venn diagrams — Juvenile literature. 2. Charts, diagrams, etc. — Juvenile literature.
3. Mathematical analysis — Juvenile literature.
I. Harasymiw, Therese. II. Title.
QA248.3 H37 2015
511—d23

Published in 2015 by
Gareth Stevens Publishing
111 East 14th Street, Suite 349
New York, NY 10003

Copyright © 2015 Gareth Stevens Publishing

Designer: Katelyn E. Reynolds
Editor: Therese Shea

Photo credits: Cover, p. 1 (Venn diagram) John T Takai/Shutterstock.com; cover, pp. 1–24 (background texture) ctrlaplus/Shutterstock.com; pp. 5, 7, 9, 11, 13, 15, 17, 19, 21 (Venn diagram elements) Colorlife/Shutterstock.com; p. 15 (photo) Blend Images/Shutterstock.com; p. 17 (photo) poonsap/Shutterstock.com.

Printed in the United States of America

CPSIA compliance information: Batch #CS15GS: For further information contact Gareth Stevens, New York, New York at 1-800-542-2595.

Contents

Boldface words appear in the glossary.

Sets

In math, the word for two or more things that are connected in some way is "set." For example, a set of odd numbers might be: 1, 3, 5, 7. A set of red rectangles might look like the ones on the next page.

set

In the Circle

In a Venn **diagram**, each set is placed in a circle. The circle is **labeled** to help you understand what's inside. Sometimes, two sets have things in common. This is shown in the area where the circles **overlap**.

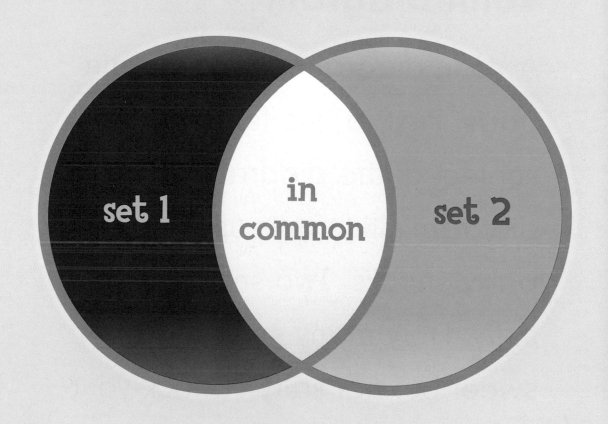

set 1

in
common

set 2

7

The Parts of a Venn Diagram

A Venn diagram needs certain parts. First, a title tells what the subject of the diagram is. This diagram's title tells us it's about party snacks. Two snacks are salty. How many snacks are sweet but *not* salty? Check your answer on page 22.

8

Party Snacks

salty
2

both
1

sweet
3

9

Each circle in the Venn diagram should have a label. Look at these labels. They tell you that some of the bugs in the jar have wings and some are green. How many bugs have wings *and* are green?

Bugs in the Jar

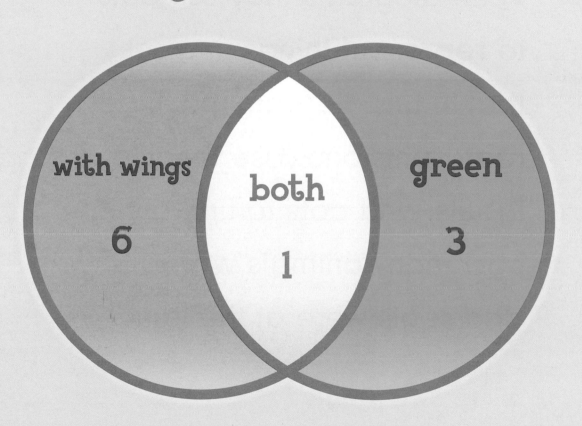

with wings
6

both
1

green
3

Venn diagrams may use dots to **represent** things in a set, too. In this diagram, each dot represents one. Use the title, labels, and dots to find out how many animals with tails _and_ spots were at the fair.

Animals at the Fair

Diagramming the Band

Imagine you're thinking about putting together a band. You want to make a Venn diagram to show what musical **instruments** your friends play. First, draw 2 circles on a piece of paper. Make sure they overlap.

15

Next, write your title and label your circles. You may want friends who can play guitar and drums in your band. So, let's use the title "What Do They Play?" Label the circles "guitar" and "drums."

What Do They Play?

guitar   both   drums

17

Imagine three friends only play the guitar and five friends only play the drums. Two friends play both the guitar and drums. Now, put the dots in the correct place in your Venn diagram. It should look like the one here.

What Do They Play?

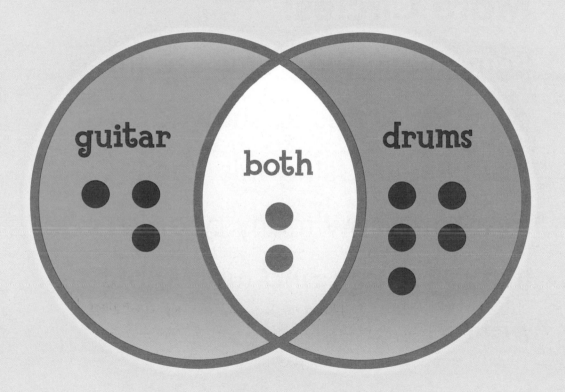

More Circles!

Some Venn diagrams use three or more circles to show facts about sets. Using this Venn diagram, how many people like alligators *and* turtles, but *not* crocodiles?

Our Favorite Animals

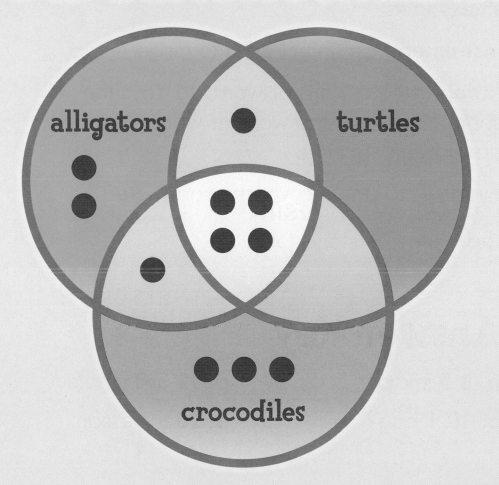

Glossary

diagram: a chart, graph, or drawing that shows facts

instrument: an object used to make music

label: using a word or words to describe something. Also, the word or words used to describe something.

overlap: to partly cover the same area

represent: to stand for

Answer Key

p. 8 3 snacks

p. 10 1 bug

p. 12 5 animals

p. 20 1 person

For More Information

Books

Boswell, Kelly. *Diagrams, Diagrams, Diagrams!* North Mankato, MN: Capstone Press, 2014.

Dowdy, Penny. *Graphing*. New York, NY: Crabtree Publishing, 2008.

Websites

Venn Diagram
www.readwritethink.org/files/resources/interactives/venn_diagrams/
Use this site to make a Venn diagram online.

Venn Diagrams
www.ixl.com/math/grade-2/interpret-venn-diagrams
Test your understanding by answering questions about Venn diagrams.

Venn Diagrams
www.purplemath.com/modules/venndiag.htm
Read how to use a Venn diagram to put animals in sets.

Index